I-SPY

with David Bellamy

BRITISH WILDLIFE

I-Spy Books
12 Star Road, Partridge Green
Horsham, Sussex RH13 8RA

COME ON ALL I-SPYERS, HERE IS A REAL CHALLENGE!

Of all the I-Spy books this will probably be the most tricky to complete. Why? Because much of our wildlife is very shy and retiring—and who can blame them when you remember how badly some of us humans behave.

To deserve your Wildlife Observer I-Level Order of Merit you are going to have to go into the country, keep quite quiet and have a lot of patience. However, many of the animals in the book can be seen in the urban sprawl around even our largest towns. Why, I saw a fox with a black rat in its mouth walking through Soho in the middle of London not long ago!

SCORING

As you spot each of the animals in this book – and answer the simple question – you earn an I-SPY score. When your scores total 1250 points you may award yourself the rank of WILDLIFE OBSERVER with Silver Honours. When they reach a complete total of 1500 points you are entitled to the rank of WILDLIFE OBSERVER with Gold Honours; you may then send your book to me, and I shall return it to you stamped with my personal seal. Your certificate of rank is on the inside-back-cover of this book.

Good luck!

HOW TO OBSERVE

When you start looking for these animals remember that you will probably find, first of all, traces of where they have been; teethmarks on remains of their food, for instance, and their tracks.

Most animals have sharper senses than ours – they need them in order to survive. So to see them in their natural surroundings you must be very quiet, very patient, and make use of cover and prevailing wind. Stand still – or sit still; then look, with binoculars if possible, and listen. Then you will find how exciting it is to watch the wild animals that share this country with us.

HOW TO KEEP TRACK

First off, what visits your garden? If you have had the builder in, and with permission from Dad and Mum, you might put down a Track Track, along the edge of the lawn, close to the garden border. A Track Track consists of a strip of sand 10–20 cms wide, about 2 metres long and no more than 2 cms deep. You may well be surprised at the tracks that are left by the animals who visit the bottom of your garden.

KEEPING A GOOD TRACK RECORD

Drawings or photos will do, but a permanent 3-D record can be made as follows. You will need: plaster of paris (from a DIY shop), a strip of cardboard and a paper-clip. Press the cardboard into the ground round the print, and pour in a creamy mixture of plaster. Leave at least one hour, then dig it out, clean it up, identify and label.

Score for 6 good track records. *What have you recorded?* .... Score **60**

Moles and mole hills The hills first, as they're easy to find – mounds of freshly turned earth, about 20 cms across, dotted about in woods, fields, perhaps across your lawn, and even on motorway embankments. As a mole digs its tunnel it needs to put all the loosened soil somewhere, so, every so often, it bores upwards and dumps it at the surface.

Moles are found all over mainland Britain, but not in Ireland. They feed mainly on earthworms, needing half their own body weight in food each day. Young are usually four in number and born in an underground nest in April.

How far apart were the mole hills you saw? .... Score **15**
Where did you see a mole? .... Score **50**

Hedgehog Active at night, hunting slugs and snails, worms and insects, so look for them as they set out at dusk. If alarmed a hedgehog rolls into a spiny ball – good protection except to a determined fox or badger. A spiny coat is difficult to preen, so carries many fleas; but they are hedgehog fleas, not interested in humans or our pets.

Usually five blind babies with soft white spines are born in early summer. After 36 hours sharp dark spines show, and their eyes open in a fortnight. There may be a second litter. Leave a saucer of milk on the lawn and you may be visted by a mother and her piglets! They hibernate, surviving on fat built up from heavy autumn feeding.

On what date did you see a hedgehog? ....
.... Score **30**

Shrews are insectivores, related to the mole and hedgehog. They hunt constantly to eat their own weight in food every 24 hours, and will die if without food for four hours. They do not hibernate. You may see a dead one, caught perhaps by a cat but then dropped because of the nasty smell from its scent glands. Owls, with no sense of smell, eat them.

The **Common Shrew**, 12 cms long including tail, has light fur along its sides. The 9 cms long **Pygmy Shrew**, grey-brown above and pale below, is the only kind also found in Ireland. A larger, black and white shrew, swimming, is the **Water Shrew**.

I-SPYed a shrew on .... Score **40**

Hedgehog

Common Shrew (left) and Pygmy Shrew

Bats are the only mammals that can really fly. There are some 750 fascinating species around the world, and a dozen in Britain.

Ours appear mainly at night, feeding on flying insects. To locate in darkness branches, telephone wires and other objects like you and me that are to be avoided, and food that is to be caught, bats have a system of echo-location, like radar. They send out ultrasonic squeaks, up to 200 a second, and pick up the tiny echoes that bounce back off things. You will probably be able to hear some of their lower-frequency squeaks; as you get older you'll lose the ability.

Identifying night-flying bats can be difficult, so let's concentrate on just three: the biggest, the smallest, and one with long ears!

Noctule About 35 cms span, a big high-flier in open wooded areas, often emerging before sunset to replace swifts. Fast swooping flight and loud squeaks. Will pouch a big insect in its tail until ready to eat it. Not in Ireland.

Pipistrelle About 18 cms span, our smallest and commonest. A fast, twisting flier, often around houses and seen soon after sunset.

Long-eared Bat About 24 cms span, and comes out later. Hovers quite low round trees, often picking insects off leaves.

Which did you see and where? .... Score **45**

Bats *are* fascinating, and they *won't* get themselves caught in ladies' hair if they can possibly help it!

Top: Noctule, centre: Long-eared, bottom: Pipistrelle bat

Rabbits and **Hares** are not rodents. They differ in having a second pair of upper gnawing teeth behind the front ones.

The Rabbit is a plump, grey-brown animal with a short fluffy white tail. A burrow-dweller, it can be seen grazing during the day but is most active after dusk. Not a native, it was brought to Britain by the Normans. Many mammals and birds hunt rabbits, but they survive by having several litters a year, each averaging six blind, helpless babies. They are independent at three weeks.

In what kind of country did you see rabbits? .... Score **30**

Hares are solitary animals, except in spring when they gather to fight and chase in courtship ('Mad March Hares'). They live above ground, resting in a shallow scrape called a form. Each year there will be three or four litters of two or three babies called leverets, born with fur and open eyes. Placed by the doe in separate forms, they are independent after a week.

The **Brown Hare** is large and dark brown with long ears and legs. Its white tail is black on top and the ears have black tips. The long hind legs make it faster uphill than down, and it can reach 70 kph. Introduced in Ireland.

The **Blue Hare** or **Mountain Hare,** found in Ireland and upland north Britain, especially Scotland, is smaller, with shorter ears and no black on the tail. In the north it may turn white in winter.

Where did you see a hare? .... Score **45**

Now for the true rodents, and around the world they make up more than a third of all mammal species.

Red Squirrel Rare, found in coniferous forests where it eats the seeds from cones, plus bark, leaves and some animal food like insects and birds' eggs. About 40 cms long including tail, it makes domed nests called dreys, and two or three babies are born in spring. The ear tufts are seen only in winter, when the tail turns very pale in colour.

Grey Squirrel Bigger, about 48 cms long, and introduced from N. America 100 years ago. It prefers deciduous woods, and has driven the Red Squirrel from this habitat. Now seen even in inner city parks, it eats fruits, seeds, buds and fungi, robs birds' nests and is especially fond of acorns. SPY it burying them in autumn for winter use (it usually forgets where they are!). Like its relative it builds a drey and does not hibernate.

Where did you see which squirrel? ....
.... Score Grey **30** and Red **65**

Fat Dormouse Another introduction, but much more localised – from Europe to the Chiltern Hills in southern England. Looking like a small Grey Squirrel 30 cms long, it feeds at night in the tops of woods and orchards, and hibernates in a nest that might be in a hollow tree or even an attic.

Dormouse Only 15 cms long, these beautiful little furry tailed animals are also nocturnal, and

Grey and red squirrels

Fat Dormouse   Dormouse

hibernate – sometimes in a bird box. They like a tangle of brambles and wild honeysuckle to feed and nest in, and are mainly found in the south and west.

Where did you see your dormouse? ....
.... Score **65**

Voles are plump little rodents, very different from mice, with small ears, blunt heads and shortish tails. They do not hibernate, and are top of the menu for birds, mammals and snakes.

Bank Vole Small, reddish-brown with a moderate tail that is darker on top. A good climber, it is often to be seen in daylight working its way through undergrowth.

Short-tailed Vole Another small, round animal, with an even shorter tail. Grey-brown, with very small ears. It prefers grassland and runs rather than climbs. SPY its network of runways by gently pulling back grass tussocks. Like the Bank Vole it is a noisy chatterer, but unlike it it makes a nest at the ground surface; the Bank Vole burrows underground a few centimetres. Populations of Short-tailed Voles occasionally swell dramatically in numbers, but are quickly controlled by bird and mammal predators.

Water Vole At 30 cms this is the largest of the European species, often called a water rat, which it isn't. Look for it along slow streams, canals and dykes, especially at dawn or dusk when it is most active. All sorts of waterside plants are eaten, and grass stems are a particular favourite. SPY burrow entrances in the banks. There will be others under water. These voles are good swimmers and divers, paddling with all four feet. In winter you may be lucky enough to see one swimming under the ice!

When and where did you see any of these three? ....
.... Score **35**

Have you a mouse about the house? Well, that will probably be the ordinary **House Mouse**, which seems to have been living alongside us human beings ever since Stone Age times. But, just to be awkward, two of our wild outdoor mice often come indoors, especially in the country.

Wood Mouse or **Long-tailed Field Mouse** At 20 cms it is bigger than the House Mouse (17 cms) and lighter in colour. It has a small yellow patch between the forelegs. It lives in open country, hedgerows and gardens, emerging at night for whatever is going. In summer buds, insects, snails and earthworms; in winter an underground nut store. It does not hibernate, and breeds at any time though usually not before February, nesting sometimes in an old bird's nest.

Yellow-necked Mouse Also a nocturnal food-storer. 2 cms longer but very similar. Its yellow patch is bigger, forming a collar, and it prefers woodland in its southern British range. An excellent climber, of trees and also house walls – it is very fond of apples stored in lofts!

Harvest Mouse The only mammal in Europe with a prehensile tail that it can use as a fifth foot as it scuttles up and down stems, day and night. Modern agricultural methods mean it breeds less in cornfields, but look out for its spherical nest of grasses in hedgerows. It spends the winter in undergrowth at ground level.

I-SPYed an outdoor mouse on .... Score **35**

Wood Mouse (left) and Yellow-necked Mouse

Harvest Mouse

Two kinds of rats are found in Britain, both originally from Asia and brought in by accident. The **Black Rat** or **Ship Rat** may have arrived with the returning Crusaders in the Middle Ages. It is the smaller, with longer ears and tail and usually darker fur, living in cities generally close to ports. It spread the Great Plague of London in 1665.

The Brown Rat, about 44 cms long, came in the 18th century from a more northerly home and is much hardier. It ousted the Black Rat from much of its range and is now found in colonies everywhere, in town and country. There may be over a dozen young in a litter. Anything is eaten by these very intelligent animals, but grain for preference.

Where did you see a rat? .... Score **20**

Coypu Another introduced menace! This big web-footed aquatic animal from South America was bred here for fur in the 1930s, and some escaped. Twenty years later it was all over East Anglia, breaching river banks with its burrows and destroying crops. The same thing happened many years ago with musk rats, but these were all caught and have now disappeared. The coypu is more of a problem and seems to be holding its own. I-SPY a large animal 90 cms long with bright orange incisor teeth. It is related to the porcupine.

Where did you see your coypu? ....
.... Score **55**

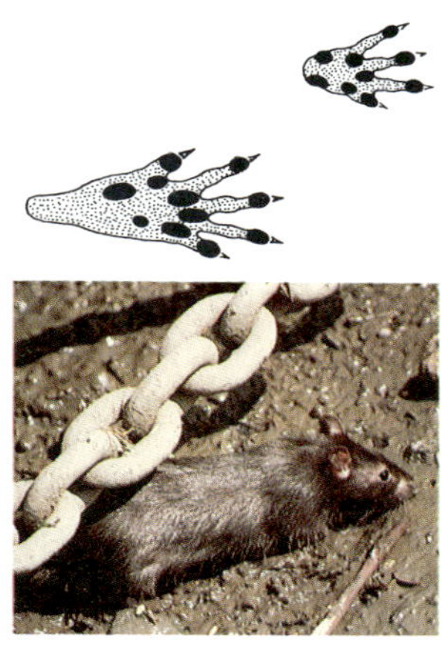

Black Rat (left) and Brown Rat

The **Fox** is our next largest carnivore after the badger, and perhaps the best known. A resourceful animal, full of cheek and a real pest. I-SPY a rusty-brown animal with pricked ears, sharp muzzle and long thick tail or 'brush', about 1.2 metres overall. Foxes are everywhere, even in cities and towns where they raid dustbins and backyard hen runs, and snatch the occasional cat. Country foxes prefer rodents.

Dog fox and vixen start running together in late autumn, and it is at this time of year that you may hear the harsh yelp of a vixen, a high-pitched sound starting on a low note then rising. You may hear the dog fox answer with a sharp double bark.

Foxes take advantage of other creatures' labours when looking for a home, perhaps enlarging old rabbit burrows or sharing part of a badger's sett. Sometimes the family takes up quarters in rubbish tips, under old mattresses and corrugated iron.

A month or so after the cubs are born in March or April the dog fox leaves the earth and the vixen becomes teacher and provider of food, often moving the cubs to new quarters if disturbed.

Score for seeing any spot where a fox has been, or its hole, or the remains of its meal.

What else have you discovered about the fox for yourself? ....
....
.... Score **50**

More carnivores, and from our only wild dog to some members of the weasel family. The two smallest first, **Stoat** and **Weasel**. How to tell them apart? Well, the stoat is stoatally different and the weasel is weasely distinguishable!

Actually the **Stoat** always has a black tip to its tail, and is larger – 35 cms long. Found all over Britain, in the north it may turn white (keeping its black tail tip) in winter – the ermine fur used in robes. A fierce little hunter of rats and voles, it will climb to birds' nests and daze a rabbit by dancing round it until close enough to pounce on this much larger animal.

I-SPYed a stoat on .... Score **40**

The **Weasel**, 27 cms long and with a smaller, single colour tail, is not found in Ireland. Like its cousin it is a climber and a swimmer, and its smaller size lets it chase voles along their undergrass and underground runways, so these are its chief food. It does not turn winter white in Britain. Like the stoat it is mostly nocturnal but often seen dashing about by day, pausing to rear on hind legs to keep watch. Two litters of four or five may be raised, in a nest tucked away among tree roots or in a stone wall. The stoat has a single larger litter. Both of these attractive little terrors are found right the way across Europe *and* Asia *and* North America!

Where have you seen a weasel? ....
.... Score **40**

One doesn't think of a **Badger** as a weasel, but they are in the same Mustelid family (along with the martens, otter and mink). It's our biggest carnivore, about 85 cms long and 15 kilos in weight. Nocturnal, it can best be seen emerging at dusk for a night hunting insects, slugs and snails, frogs, plants and, especially, earthworms. Like foxes, some are taking to overturning dustbins for our throwaways, but only in country areas. If your garden carrots are mysteriously vanishing overnight, that could well be a badger!

Big holes in a bank, each with a pile of excavated earth in front, lead into a network of tunnels called a sett. After an inactive (but not hibernating) winter, up to five young are born in a breeding chamber at the end of a tunnel in early February. Blind at birth, they stay below for two months before venturing out to play at night under the eye of the sow. They may live for 10 or more years.

Badgers are very widespread (though not numerous) in wooded areas around Britain, and I hope you're lucky enough to see one of these handsome animals one moonlit night. You might SPY one when you're least expecting to - caught in the car headlights as it grubs around in a lay-by litter bin!

Score for either badger or sett. Where did you see what? ....
....
.... Score **65**

The badger is a very clean animal. He grooms himself regularly, combing his back and stomach with his long claws. He changes the bedding from his set regularly and buries any rubbish. If you SPY any remains, for example chicken feathers, it is more likely that a fox is using the set.

Like the badger and fox, the **Otter** is mainly nocturnal. This, plus its ability to dive for up to four minutes and swim with only the nose and high-mounted eyes showing, makes it difficult to see. And though they are widespread (river, lake, estuary and coast), otters are rare. Polluted rivers, 'tidied' banks and other human disturbance have reduced their numbers. So: if you see one, do not disturb; and you may score for seeing only signs of otters.

Their den, or holt, is usually under the roots of a waterside tree, and a litter of two or three is usually born in early summer. Strangely, young otters dislike water and have to be led – or pushed! – by their mother. Young and old are very playful, and make slides down banks in mud or snow. Look for these, and prints of its well webbed feet. Slow-swimming (and sickly) fish, crabs and eels are taken, also rodents, frogs, insects and waterbirds. Up to 1.2 metres long, it is found across Europe, Asia and North America.

What did you see, when and where? ....
.... Score **80**

Now another foreign escaper that is increasing along our waterways, the **American Mink**. About 55 cms long and usually dark brown, it is not so aquatic as the otter, preferring to jump on fish from the bank. Also eats rodents, birds.

What did you see, when and where? ....
.... Score **50**

Seals are related to carnivores, and evolved from them as specialist sea-dwellers about 15 million years ago. Well streamlined, with no external ears, their legs are adapted as flippers – the front for steering and the rear turned backwards for powerful swimming.

Two species are native to Britain, and the greater part of the world's population of one, the **Grey Seal**, come ashore to breed on our rocky north and west coasts. Pups are born in late autumn and after three weeks lose their white coat, begin to swim and are on their own. The big bull seals, up to 3 metres long, fight each other to establish territory for their wives. In early spring all go back to the sea again. Often only their heads are visible, as they rest in a vertical position. Food is mainly fish, and they can stay under for 20 minutes!

The **Common Seal** is about 1.6 metres long, prefers shallow waters and flat sands, so is to be seen on the east coast too, around estuaries. In early summer they haul out on sandbanks at low tide to give birth, and the pups are able to swim as the tide returns. Like the grey seal they are active during the day, and can dive for 15 minutes. (Best of all is the **Harp Seal**, a very rare visitor from the Arctic pack ice, which can dive to a depth of 260 metres and hold its breath for half an hour!).

Which seal did you see, and where and when?
.... Score **65**

Above: Grey
Seal

Above:
Common
Seal

Harp Seal

Deer, like cattle, have evolved the ability to gobble down food fast and then, later on, in a sheltered spot away from the danger of wolves and other predators, to bring it up again and chew it properly for digestion - chewing the cud.

The **Red Deer** is our largest. A stag can stand 1.3 metres high at the shoulder and weigh 200 kilos. Really a woodland animal, they have adapted in Scotland to high open country. Outside parks they can be wary, but they are quite widespread on moors and in forests and, though basically nocturnal, can often be seen from a road, far away on a high hill or closer on a New Forest heath.

Calves are born singly in May or June and lie up for a week in undergrowth, camouflaged by their spotted coat. After a month they join the herd of hinds. Stags stay apart, but come together in October to fight for the herd. Their challenging roar carries a long way.

Only stags have antlers, and during its first year a stag has only a single small spike. But thereafter each year's new set grows bigger and with more tines (points), before being shed every February. When the two antlers each have six tines the stag is called a 'royal' and the tines have names: 'brow, bay, trey and three atop'. Red deer feed on grasses, tree shoots and bark.

Where did you see Red Deer? ....

What interested you most about them? ....
.... Score **50**

The **Fallow Deer**, from the Mediterranean area, was probably brought here by the Normans. Like most deer only the males, called bucks, have antlers, which while growing are covered in hairy skin called velvet. Fallow antlers are palmate in shape and are cast (dropped) in May-June. It is 90 cms at the shoulder, this is a widespread woodland and park deer, usually with a spotted coat that moults to dull grey-brown in winter. There is a very pale form and one that is dark coated (Epping Forest near London has some). Often, all you will see of deer is their back ends as they slip quietly away into cover. Luckily, a sure way to identify all kinds, whatever their colour form, with or without antlers, is the colour pattern of their rumps.

How many Fallow Deer were in your herd? .... Score **50**

The smaller **Roe Deer**, 70 cms at the shoulder, is a native, very widespread in woods and copses with good cover. It is less sociable than others, generally being seen in ones or twos. Note the small antlers. They are cast in early winter and regrown by April. Winter and summer coats are different in colour. New-born fallow fawns and roe kids are kept hidden in dense bracken by the doe, who stays close by. Roes often have twins, but usually only one survives.

When and where did you see your Roe? ....
.... Score **55**

Now for three east Asian introduced species that have become widespread in the wild. Smallest of all, a dear little deer only 50 cms at the shoulder, is the **Muntjac**. They are solitary, keep to dense woodland and are difficult to see, but their sharp bark, repeated every few seconds, carries far. Their tiny antlers are set on furry pedicles, they are leaf-browsers and fruit eaters and produce a fawn at any time, usually twice a year.

Nearly as small, at 60 cms, is the **Chinese Water Deer**. Wide-ranging in woods especially near reedy marshes, these strange little animals never bear antlers. Instead, the bucks' upper canine teeth are elongated into little tusks. Like muntjac they eat leaves and fruits but breed only in May–June, often giving birth to three or four fawns.

Much bigger is the **Sika Deer**, only a few cms smaller than the fallow. Another woodlander, but this one prefers to stay in small herds. It is related to the red deer and has similar antlers, but its autumn call is very different – a light bark rising in pitch to a loud whistle. Most of ours came from Japan.

If you are lucky enough to come across a cast antler of any kind it will probably have its owner's own tooth marks on it – getting back some of the minerals to build the next pair.

What have you seen or heard of these three? ...
....
.... Score **60**

Top: Muntjac, Centre: Chinese Water Deer, Above: Sika
Deer

You may score for certain fascinating primitive sorts of domestic animals, running more or less free, that closely resemble their wild ancestors: sheep on small islands, goats in craggy uplands and big-horned white cattle in parks. There are eight regional breeds of ponies, from Shetland in the north to New Forest (see inside-front-cover) in the south; the Exmoor is reckoned to be the most ancient of all.
What did you see where? ....
.... Score **40**

Far older than seals, **Whales** began evolving from land mammals 50 million years ago. **Porpoise** and **Dolphins**, small, toothed whales catching fish by echo-location, are the sorts you'll most likely see round our coasts, whether on a boat trip or SPYing from cliff tops (careful!).

Common Porpoise (A) is now rare in the North Sea but may be seen on other coasts. Up to 2 metres long, it doesn't usually leap clear of the water. **Common Dolphin** (B), about the same size, swims fast in large 'schools', often leaping clear to show the yellow patch. Mainly in the south and west. **Bottle-nosed Dolphin** (C) is larger, over 3 metres, and in smaller schools in the English Channel and the west. **White-beaked Dolphin** (D), rarer, more likely in the North Sea in schools of over 1500. Often becomes stranded on beaches. Over 3 metres long. **White-sided Dolphin** (E) is 2.5 metres long and rare. Most likely in the north and west.
What did you see where? ....
.... Score **65**

(A)
(B)
(C)
(D)
(E)

British amphibians and reptiles are becoming so rare that it is now against the law to sell any of them, and some may not even be handled. They have every right to live here, just as we do, so: look out for them and enjoy observing them, but let them lead their own little lives, please!

Newts spend a lot of time on land, hunting small creepy crawlies in moist places like leafy ditches or under logs. In spring they move to still fresh water to breed. Eggs are laid singly and hatch into tadpoles with gills. Legs develop, the gills disappear and the young newts leave the water. All have orangey spotted bellies and are more brightly marked when breeding, the males growing crests. Of our three newts only the first is found in Ireland.

The **Smooth Newt** on land is a plain little animal 11 cms long and spotted below. In the water the breeding male grows a beautiful crest and spots all over.

The **Palmate Newt**, smallest at 9 cms, likes clear peaty water and ranges high on moors. The male has webbed hind feet and a thread-like tail tip.

The big (14 cms) **Warty** or **Crested Newt** is a Specially Protected Species, not to be disturbed. It often remains in the water after the breeding season.

Which did you see, where and when? ....
....
.... Score **35**

Smooth Newt

Crested Newt male (top) and female

Only three newts, one frog and two toads are native to Britain, compared with many more on the Continent. Why? Have a think about it.

Common Frog (A) – but less so as ponds are filled in everywhere. 50 points straight away if you have (or will make) a pond in your garden and encourage amphibians to breed in it - they'll find it! Frogs come twice to water, once in spring to spawn and again in autumn to hibernate on the bottom. There may be 4000 eggs in each female's spawn, and tadpoles are valuable food for many small animals from dragonfly larvae to water shrews. As frogs they are hunted especially by grass snakes, and many mammals and birds.

What colour was your frog? .... Score **30**

Common Toad (B). Like (A) varies its colour to suit its surroundings. I-SPY its dry, warty skin and shorter legs – it walks rather than hops, and lies up in dryer spots before coming out at night after insects, etc, especially ants. Returns year after year in masses to a particular breeding pond, travelling a kilometre or more by night and passing other ponds on the way that seem just as suitable.

Natterjack Toad (C). Another Specially Protected Species, only 7–8 cms long and easily recognized by its back stripe and its running gait. A very rare heath and duneland dweller.

Which toad did you see and where? ....
.... Score **35**

(A)

(B)   (C)

The Common Lizard is also called the **Viviparous Lizard,** meaning live-bearing. Instead of laying eggs, with the risk that they may be eaten, or chill, the mother basking in the sun keeps them in her body, in their egg sacs, until they are ready to hatch. Then, in July–August, 8–10 fully mobile lizardlets are born. About 15 cms long it can be found almost anywhere from ditches to heaths to woods and hills. The only reptile in Ireland. It feeds almost entirely on insects and (like all our reptiles) hibernates, from October to April. Our lizards have the ability to shed their tail if it is grabbed by a predator. It even continues to wriggle for a while! A replacement will grow, but this takes much protein and it is never as long.

The **Sand Lizard** is another very rare Specially Protected Species that lives on a few of our fast disappearing heaths and dunes. A dozen soft-shelled eggs are buried to hatch in these warm places by themselves in midsummer.

Slow-worm Not a snake but a legless *lizard* (so it has eyelids). 30–40 cms long and widely found along field and wood edges and waste ground where there is cover. Feeds on slugs and earthworms and the silver or gold babies are born free in August–September. Sheds its skin in pieces, not whole as snakes do.

Describe where you saw a slow-worm .... Score **40**

On what kind of ground did you see a lizard? ... . Score **40**

Many amphibians and reptiles on the Continent, a mere 12 in the British Isles. Why? Well, most of Britain went under the ice during the last Ice Age, and such creatures simply went south, there being no English Channel in the way. Then the climate warmed, the ice melted, the seas rose and we were cut off – before many species had moved north again.

Grass Snake Our commonest and largest, up to 90 cms. Often seen near water for its diet of amphibians and fish; a good swimmer. I-SPY its pale yellow collar. Completely harmless, but may discharge an evil-smelling fluid if handled. Eggs may be laid in a compost heap or haystack for warmth. The **Adder** or **Viper** is venomous, and may bite in self-defence if molested. Leave it alone and it will quickly slip away. I-SPY a short thick snake 50–60 cms long, tapering suddenly at the tail; a zigzag and blotches pattern with a 'V' on the head. A live-bearer, likes dry places – open, woodland or coastal, and hunts small mammals and lizards. **Smooth Snake** A slenderer 60 cms snake, right at the edge of its range on the few south of England heaths where it is found. Harmless, and a very rare Specially Protected Species only identified here in 1853. I-SPY (if you are very lucky) the dark line through the eye, and less of a neck than the other snakes. Its main diet is lizards.

Where and when did you see what snake? ....
.... Score **50**

Good news for wildlife (and Wildlife Observers) is that there are lots of conservation areas in Britain where our wild animals and plants are specially looked after. From big National Parks and National Nature Reserves down to smaller local areas, they are good SPYing places. But *please* obey the rules at each one you visit.

Which conservation area did you go to and what was your best wildlife sighting there? .... Score **40**

The badges of three societies of interest to you. Send a stamp for details.

You can find out about species and visit local and national reserves by joining **WATCH**, 22 The Green, Nettleham, Lincoln LN2 2NR.

The Mammal Society, 41 Hatherley Road, Reading, Berks. RG1 5QE, has a junior section and organizes meetings and summer camps.

The **Young People's Trust for Endangered Species** is mostly organized through a teacher at school, and with activities and lectures covers both our own and worldwide wildlife. YPTES, 19 Quarry Street, Guildford, Surrey GU1 3EH.

JOIN THE I-SPY CLUB

- All you need to join the I-SPY Club is to buy a Membership Book which includes the secret codes. Ask at your bookshop or newsagent.

- Tell your friends about I-SPY. Invite them to join and form a Patrol with you.

- Collect all the I-SPY books—and you'll have a wonderful library of your own.

- Write to me about any interesting discoveries you make. You may win a prize! Remember to enclose a stamped addressed envelope for a reply.

*LOOK OUT FOR THESE I-SPY WITH
DAVID BELLAMY BOOKS*

AT THE AIRPORT
ARCHAEOLOGY
AT THE ART
   GALLERY
BIRDS AND
   REPTILES AT
    THE ZOO
BRITISH COINS
BRITISH WILDLIFE
ON A CAR
   JOURNEY
CAR NUMBERS
CARS
CIVIL AIRCRAFT
CREEPY CRAWLIES

DINOSAURS
FISH AND
   FISHING
FRUITS AND
   FUNGI
GARDEN FLOWERS
   ALL THE YEAR
    ROUND
GARDEN BIRDS
MAMMALS AT THE
   ZOO
ON A TRAIN
   JOURNEY
TREES
WILD FLOWERS

AND MANY **MORE!** TO COME

INDEX

ACKNOWLEDGEMENTS

Illustrations Anthony Maynard, pp 5, 9, 27, 37, and pawprints. Photos: G. Kinns/BioFotos, pp 19 (top right), 21 (bottom). J. M. Terhune/Biofotos, p 29 (centre). Heather Angel, pp 25, 43 (top and bottom), 45 (top). Press-Tige Pictures, pp 13, 15, 19 (top left and bottom), 21 (top), 29 (top and bottom), 33, 39 (top), 41, 43 (centre), 45 (centre and bottom). *Shell Times*, page 2.
Series Editor Anthony Maynard.

Published by Ravette Limited, 12 Star Road, Partridge Green, Horsham, West Sussex RH13 8RA.
© Ravette Ltd. 1984.
Printed by Brown, Knight & Truscott Ltd, Tonbridge, Kent
ISBN 0 906710 47 2